Saving

By the same author
Debt

Idea & Concept: **Juliane Otterbach**
Text: **Samantha Downes**
Psychology Chapter: **Monika Heller**
Illustration: **Flora Douville**

Commissioning Editor: **Georgina Laycock**
Production: **Otterbach & Partners Ltd**
Design: *Dear Dad,* **Matthias Megyeri**
Editor: **Lucinda Hawksley**
Editorial Assistant: **Kira Hesser**
Consulting Editor: **Anthony Pearson**

Juliane Otterbach

Saving

ALLEN LANE
an imprint of
PENGUIN BOOKS

ALLEN LANE

Published by the Penguin Group
Penguin Books Ltd, 80 Strand, London WC2R 0RL, England
Penguin Group (USA) Inc., 375 Hudson Street, New York, New York 10014, USA
Penguin Group (Canada), 90 Eglinton Avenue East, Suite 700, Toronto,
Ontario, Canada M4P 2Y3 (a division of Pearson Penguin Canada Inc.)
Penguin Ireland, 25 St Stephen's Green, Dublin 2, Ireland
(a division of Penguin Books Ltd)
Penguin Group (Australia), 250 Camberwell Road, Camberwell,
Victoria 3124, Australia (a division of Pearson Australia Group Pty Ltd)
Penguin Books India Pvt Ltd, 11 Community Centre,
Panchsheel Park, New Delhi – 110 017, India
Penguin Group (NZ), 67 Apollo Drive, Rosedale, North Shore 0632, New Zealand
(a division of Pearson New Zealand Ltd)
Penguin Books (South Africa) (Pty) Ltd, 24 Sturdee Avenue,
Rosebank, Johannesburg 2196, South Africa

Penguin Books Ltd, Registered Offices: 80 Strand, London WC2R 0RL, England

www.penguin.com

First published 2008
1

Copyright © Juliane Otterbach, 2008

The moral right of the author has been asserted

Set in Corporate E
Printed in Italy by Graphicom, srl

A CIP catalogue record for this book is available from the British Library

ISBN: 978–1–846–14098–3

Legal Disclaimer
We want to empower people to get an overview of their finances and learn about
the options they have. However, this book is in no way meant to replace a financial
adviser. We strongly recommend that you seek the opinion of an independent
financial adviser who understands your particular circumstances before embarking
on drastically new strategies with your finances. As publisher Penguin cannot
accept liability for any loss which you may suffer as a result of following the
suggestions contained in this book.
All website links set out in this book were correct at the time of going to press.
The author and the publisher cannot take any responsibility for content appearing
on third party websites.

Contents

Introduction

What's your next treat going to be? The latest gaming console, an exotic pet or getting your teeth whitened? With such delights dangled in front of you, it's easy to lose sight of what will happen once your working years are over.

If you have been neglecting your financial future, you're not alone. **Over 40 per cent of people in the UK don't have a personal pension and 70 per cent admit to no significant savings. That's not good news**: with the current state of the world economy, these figures mean that many of us will be poor when we're old. We can't even rely on a state pension to bail us out as year on year the amount that the state supplies sinks lower and lower. If you don't want to spend your senior years living on catfood, you have to act now.

Financial planning will confront you with uncomfortable questions. Are you prepared for the unforeseen? What if you suddenly fall ill and can't work for a while, no jobs come along that you like, or your computer finally gives up the ghost? A financial safety cushion will give you peace of mind and carry you through temporary crises. In the same way, you need to build up something that can provide security for the rest of your life.

Having some savings not only gives you security; it also provides you with the freedom to take your life into your own hands. It means you won't have to borrow money to get by. It allows you to change career if you feel stuck in a rut, or to simply take a break from work if need be.

Of course, if saving came easily, we'd already be swimming in money. You need some discipline and a clear vision to achieve your goals. But once you get the hang of it, saving can be quite thrilling. And **you'll be amazed how easily money can grow with minimal effort on your part**.

Think of this book as a personal trainer for your wealth. We've got all kinds of clever strategies and programmes that will leave your finances fitter. We want to get you excited about saving. Whether it's fun ways to squirrel away the pennies or getting started on the stock market, remember that even a tiny nest egg can grow into something substantial. **Now's the time to buck the trend of financial apathy and take control of your future.**

Saving Behaviour

'Saving is a fine thing. Especially if your parents have done it for you.'

Winston Churchill

Since the first Roman started putting aside his denarii to buy a nice new toga, saving has been something we've all struggled with. It's something we all know we should do – 80 per cent of us say we want to save – but it seems to be something we never quite get around to doing properly. This chapter aims to explain, from a psychological point of view, why saving can be challenging – but it also shows you how understanding why might help you overcome the difficulties.

Economists have spent years analysing individual spending and saving habits and how it affects the economy on a national and global level. They have identified the notion of saving as 'passive' because it is the opposite of spending. Unfortunately, that in itself creates a problem, as most human beings are programmed to avoid being passive.

Motives for Saving

Back in the 1930s, economist John Maynard Keynes was one of the first to study people's motives for saving. He came up with eight:

1 **Precaution** – saving for a 'rainy day'

2 **Foresight** – being aware that your circumstances might change

3 **Calculation** – basically, wanting your money to earn interest

4 **Improvement** – wanting your lifestyle to get better over time

5 **Independence** – attaining the liberty of self-reliance

6 **Enterprise** – having the freedom to invest money

7 **Pride** – having something to leave to your children

8 **Avarice** – saving for saving's sake

Today precaution comes top of the chart: 30 per cent of us are driven by the fear that the future will not be rosy enough, which is pessimistic but it makes good financial sense.

Instant gratification?

A recent survey discovered that British adults' saving habits have changed radically since the 1930s. Where people once saved for sensible long-term things their bank managers would approve of, most of us are now more motivated by instant gratification and the short term. Heading the list was 'holidays' and second was 'specific purchases' (such as a new car) with 'self-gratification' and 'self-esteem' (spa weekends and even cosmetic surgery) making it into the list.

We're not all a hedonistic bunch, however. The motives Keynes identified are still relevant with a few extras, including 'old age/in case of illness', 'speculation' and 'to avoid debt'. Interestingly, 'saving as habit' sneaked in there at number seven.

What happens when we start saving?

Psychologists have conducted all kinds of studies and experiments exploring why humans do and don't save; which section of the population is most likely to do so and why it's so difficult for us to handle saving's obstruction of instant gratification.

Is saving instinctive?

In 1975, behavioural psychologist G.W. Ainslie set up an experiment in Harvard university's famous pigeon lab to examine instinctual saving habits. In the study, any pigeons that pecked a red key received food immediately. If they didn't peck it, they got even more food, but only after a few seconds. They all pecked the red key. However, when the pigeons were offered a green key that they could peck to prevent the red key from appearing and therefore always get more food, but just slightly later, a third learned to peck it.

So, if we apply these findings on self-control to ourselves, then it stands to follow that we, too, want instant gratification. If, however, we train our minds not to panic at not receiving something immediately, because we trust that if we wait a little while it'll be even better when it comes along, then we can start training ourselves to save.

Is saving schizophrenic?

In 1981, economists Hersh M. Shefrin and Richard H. Thaler developed a theory of economic self-control, which describes saving as going against the grain because it causes a conflict between our 'planner self' and our 'doer self'.

In 2004, researchers at Princeton University took their ideas further. They presented some undergraduates with a number of economic problems – which varied both in the amounts of money they were offered and the length of delays they would have to wait in order to gain interest. Throughout, their brains were being scanned to see the reactions they went through. A very interesting finding emerged: while the students were thinking about the decision, the cognitive parts of their brains showed strong activity, but when students opted to take the money immediately something else happened. In those cases, the more primitive parts of the brain, those associated with emotions and quick reactions, showed the strongest blood flow.

So we are torn between our planner and doer selves. Both operate rationally, but they have different time horizons and look at outcomes differently. The 'planner self' is concerned with usefulness for a whole lifetime and is therefore farsighted (the angel on one shoulder); whereas the 'doer self' is selfish and short-sighted (the devil in thick glasses on the other side). The planner self needs to use self-control to stop the doer self getting its own way. It's not easy to step beyond living for the moment and start planning for the future but it's worth it.

How Can We Save Better?

Most of us have good intentions, but the hard truth is that saving requires a lot of self-control. In order to change their habits, people have to start showing themselves some tough love. Successful savers plan their finances further ahead. Their strategies included:

- keeping a budgeting or house-keeping book
- not having credit cards or using cheques
- paying for everything with cash
- only ever taking a limited amount of money out with them
- transferring a certain amount to a savings account automatically each month
- returning things bought on impulse
- avoiding shopping

If you really want to start saving, it's time to cultivate willpower and restrict temptation to a minimum. There are two types of piggy banks: those with plastic lids on the bottom for easy access and those you have to actually break to reach the money. In the world of savings, to allow your preciously hoarded funds to keep accumulating, it's good if the getting is not easy.

Save This Way

Once you have overcome the reluctance to put money aside, you don't have to be like Scrooge McDuck; a little discipline will be enough to take you there. Although maybe thinking about Uncle Scrooge's daily money bath could inspire some of us to put away a bit more.

There is so much to get out of participating in your own financial success. If you set rules for yourself, you'll see your savings grow. It's like kids and cooking: when they join in the preparation for a meal they rarely, if ever, refuse to eat the result. By the same token, if you take a vested interest in your financial future, you are far more likely to relish the final result. Think of the sense of accomplishment you'll feel putting down that final payment on your retirement cottage on the Isle of Wight.

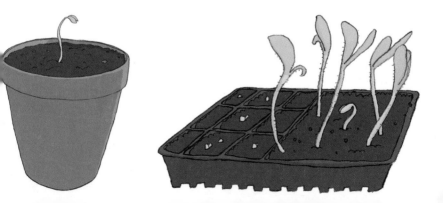

Budgeting

The unavoidable first step is getting a proper overview of your finances. Jot down all your income for the month on one side of a sheet. Then – this is harder – list your outgoings on the other side of this sheet. Start with the regular sums, like rent, heating, mobile, internet and car payments. Next work out the more ad-hoc essentials, such as food, travel costs and life's pleasures and socializing expenses (pints with friends, your iTunes downloading habit, cinema dates, etc.). And finally look at the big expenses, like any holidays you've taken and the yearly financial haemorrhage of the festive season. Now subtract the outgoings from the income and you hopefully have a little something left over. Welcome to your savings!

Once you have figured out how much you can actually afford to put aside each month in savings, you can quickly add up if this amount is going to take you anywhere or if you need more to be able to feel rich in a few years' time. If the latter is the case, you might have to look at ways to either improve your earnings or live a slightly cheaper life.

→ **www.moneymadeclear.fsa.gov.uk/tools/** – Try out the great budget calculator in this section.

→ **www.moneysavingexpert.com** – Brilliant tips to save money, regardless of age or living situation.

→ **www.moneymagpie.com** – Excellent, user-friendly site with tons of crafty tips on ways to save money as well as information on all things finance- and investment-related.

Painless Ways to Save

For most people, the difficulty lies in overcoming the reluctance to actually put that penny (or better, that tenner) aside rather than spending it right now. Therefore here is a selection of tips on how to make saving easier and ultimately let you enjoy the process, which seems to be the secret of great savers.

Out of sight, out of mind

Most hoarders set up a direct debit to a savings account that squirrels away a set sum just after payday. This is pretty painless, and leaves the rest of your income for monthly outgoings.

Savings accounts are best when they pay decent interest and make it harder to access the cash, so you won't be tempted to withdraw easily. To restrict indulging in this temptation, you can go to extremes and set up your savings account with a different bank which will delay every transfer between accounts for at least three days – thus giving you plenty of time to think over whether or not you really need that money.

There is no limitation to the number of accounts you can have. It's quite common that people have two savings accounts. One – for expensive stuff like new glasses, holidays etc. – is more of an account to hold money back in order to ensure you have it for when you want to buy something big. The second account could be an Individual Savings Account (ISA), which is tax-free. You could start paying in £50 now and if you keep paying in, in a few years' time you could be earning £100 interest per month on quite a nice tidy sum of money. The exhilarating factor is to just keep rolling over the interest and not withdrawing it, which leaves it to compound so you pile up more and more.

Now, payday can be an opportunity to add to your growing stockpile for your future – far more comforting in the long run than any new cashmere sweater.

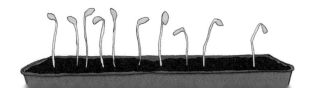

Enjoy how it grows

It's a useful habit to keep an eye on your balance. Set yourself a special time every week to check your accounts. Not only does this leave you in better control of your money, it also grants you the personal satisfaction of watching your own little garden of savings blossom.

(Warning: This gets more exciting as the risk involved in your investment increases. You may soon be elbowing all the be-suited yuppies out of the way to get to the *Financial Times* first, keen to see if your shares are soaring.)

The power of change

The old saying goes: Take care of the pence and the pounds will take care of themselves. There is something nicely old-fashioned about saving up coins. Here are three great examples of ways to make it work for you.

• Collect your loose change after each day and empty your coins into a massive jar. At the end of each month, you may have enough funds for an evening out on the lash, or for an immense family supermarket trip. If you wait until the end of the year, you can easily have saved up enough for a small holiday. By the way, the guys at your local bank will love it when you get to them dragging a suitcase full of metal money for them to count.

• Save every £2 coin you're given in change and you'll soon accumulate treasure. Rumour has it that this method has worked extremely well for some strong-minded savers who've managed to buy all sorts of lovely things, even a pair of Tiffany earrings.

• Get rid of your bad habits with this special saving therapy. For example, put a pound into a pot every time you swear. The best way is to involve the people around you as well, so you can get a little competition going.

Find your inner entrepreneur

Turn your passions/spending weaknesses into a money-making hobby. For example, if you have an enthusiasm for yoga bordering on Zen zeal, get certified and become a yoga instructor, thereby gaining access to free classes and an income from teaching. Or, if you never grew out of your action figure/comic book obsession, start collecting in a serious fashion, learn the trading racket, and earn some money from your specialist knowledge selling, trading or even offering consulting services to dealers.

Even an artistic hobby, like painting or woodwork, can turn into profit. From eBay to the smaller, handmade-design advocates at www.etsy.com, these sites allow the independent crafters to gain instant access to the public at a fraction of the price a brick-and-mortar store would cost. The immense growth of online DIY business in the past few years shows no signs of slowing. The buyer's market has shown its desire for unique, quality, handmade wares, and yours may just be the ticket to profit, all while engaging in activities that you already love.

Sort yourself out

Now that you're privy to all the tricks of the saving trade, you're at the jumping-off point for a future of great financial success. The idea is that the real secret to saving is to make it exciting, however works best, be it a self-made money box or by scoring especially good interest rates with your bank. Sure, saving loose change won't necessarily lead to a retirement cottage, but if you take all these tips and really start thinking about ways in which you can curb unnecessary spending and approach your finances in a responsible, forward-thinking way, then your future's going to be a lot easier. The very fact that you're reading this book demonstrates the desire to sort out your finances.

Banking

When they want to lure you in, banks can be a little like those bars with red leather sofas, muted lighting and a drinks list the length of *War and Peace*. They've got something to suit everyone, whether your particular poison is a pint of lager, or a chocolate fudge pomegranate martini.

Make sure you know what your lifestyle demands, be it a lenient overdraft policy or easy access to the stockmarket. When it comes to choosing a bank, there is a range of different types, each gunning for their share of the market. The secret is working out which best suits your particular needs and means and offers the best financial products.

The History of Banking

Banking has been around for much longer than the humble coin or banknote. The first banks were started in ancient Mesopotamia (now Iraq). When people wanted somewhere secure to keep their valuables – jewellery, grain, livestock, the keys to their racing chariot – they took them to their nearest royal palace or temple for safe-keeping. Eventually private house-owners got in on the act, banking began to be recognized as an industry and laws were passed to regulate it. In ancient Egypt and Greece, the taxman was paid in grain – a custom it might be worth trying to resurrect.

Banking Today

It's estimated 95 per cent of people in the UK have a bank account with a high street bank, the vast majority of which are current accounts. High street banks are huge businesses with branches and affiliations all over the world. They lend money to large companies and global institutions as well as to each other, with billions of pounds being exchanged between banks in any one day.

All high street banks are owned by shareholders. Anyone can be a shareholder; shares are listed on the stock exchange and you buy them through a stockbroker (see **Time to Play** chapter). When you buy shares you effectively own part – albeit a tiny, tiny part – of a company, along with all the other shareholders. Most people with pensions or savings plans will have unwittingly funded their pension or savings company's decision to buy shares in a high street bank.

Find out more at these websites:

→ **www.bba.org.uk** – British Bankers Association

→ **www.moneymadeclear.fsa.gov.uk** – Discover a wealth of helpful information from the Financial Services Authority

Building societies
These offer the same products as banks. Their one significant difference is that building societies are mutual companies, mostly owned by their customers.

→ **www.bsa.org.uk** – Building Societies Association

Credit unions
Credit unions work like old-fashioned Christmas clubs. All members pay in a certain amount each month and their contributions are pooled into a fund, from which members can then borrow. Credit unions often have agreements with local banks or building societies, which means their members can borrow money at a better rate than if they just walked into the bank and asked for it. Credit unions also act as matchmakers between people with money and those looking to borrow it.

Like building societies, credit unions are owned and run by their members, for their members. They are set up by people who have something in common – they might live or work in the same area, belong to the same trade union or be members of the same social club. When you first join, you'll be encouraged to save as much as you can before you are allowed to borrow.

Once you have a reliable record as a saver, you can then apply to borrow money. Unlike most financial institutions, credit unions will only let you borrow what you can afford to repay.

Having your money with a credit union is ideal if you prefer a local, ethical, co-operative way of borrowing money. Some credit unions also offer mortgages, as well as savings and current accounts.

→ **www.abcul.org** – Check out this site to find a local credit union or even set up your own.

Social Banking

There is a new breed of internet-based banks that call themselves social lenders and are ideal for people who don't want to deal with big banks. Some of them operate along the lines of a gold-diggers' dating agency. If you want to borrow money, you can go online and borrow from someone who has a bit of cash to spare. Alternatively, if you've got some spare cash and want to make some profit on it you can choose to lend it to someone and charge interest.

Although they have the same ethos as credit unions, these banks are run like private companies. The only difference is that, because it's all done privately, **borrowers don't end up paying the same kinds of interest rates they would to a bank**. In the UK the biggest social lender is called Zopa (www.zopa.com). It carries out careful credit checks so if you become a lender, your money will only be lent to credit-worthy people.

Microloans

Another new wave in social lending is microcredit, which is a relatively new concept of banking to the 'unbankable'. Very small loans, or microloans, are extended to those in poverty or who would not have otherwise been able to build up credit due to shaky employment history and lack of collateral. Since the 1970s, microloans have been especially targeted towards people living in developing countries, and have aided countless people gain steady self-employment and build up enough credit history to generate an income and a supply of wealth for themselves.

Private Banking

If you earn a lot of money, having it sit in a current account is not such a great idea. Current accounts pay lower rates of interest than savings accounts, and if you are earning thousands – or hundreds of thousands – a month, then you need access to a service whereby you don't miss out on all that juicy interest. That's when you need a private bank.

The best known private bank in the UK is Coutts, which is where the Queen has a bank account. You don't need to wear a tiara to have a private bank account, they can also be good for people who own a business or are self-employed. If you don't get paid a regular salary every month, and say, when you do get paid you tend to have a lot of money going in, it makes sense to have a more understanding bank.

Belonging to a private bank means you have access to higher rates of interest. You will also get your own private banking manager. Some private banks also provide you with a financial adviser, someone who is dedicated to making sure your money works as hard as it can.

Swiss Banking

Despite the myths, you don't need to be rich to have a Swiss Bank account. Also, despite yet more myths, it's best if you are Swiss; otherwise, unless you are an international businessman, there's little point in having one.

If, however, you've always had a hankering to be James Bond, a Swiss bank account could be an essential part of your secret identity. Swiss bank accounts are popular because, unlike most other banks, they allow you to use your cash card worldwide and make global money transfers free of charge. If you travel frequently, or deal with clients overseas, this can save you a fair amount in bank charges. (This is such a popular feature of Swiss banking that the border police have specially trained dogs to sniff out large amounts of banknotes being illegally smuggled into the country.)

Switzerland's extremely secretive banking laws mean that all the country's banks are legally obliged to keep any information about you and your account under wraps, so much so that any banker who reveals information about you risks prison. In Switzerland failure to report income or assets is not considered a crime, which means you could potentially escape paying tax in your home country, which – in the UK at least – is illegal.

Offshore Banking

All the main banks, and some building societies, offer offshore versions of savings and current accounts. They are called offshore because they are not based in the UK and are therefore subject to different kinds of taxation laws from UK-based banks. A lot of the main UK banks choose to have their offshore banking divisions in places that are not too far away from their UK headquarters, but are based where the UK tax laws don't apply, such as Jersey, the Isle of Man and Luxembourg.

Offshore banking is aimed at people who spend most of their time abroad and therefore don't have a residential status in the UK, which means they are no longer UK taxpayers. By banking offshore you are making sure the interest on savings accounts and returns from any investments can be paid to you tax-free. Be warned though, you may still have to pay tax to the government in the country where you are now living.

Savings Accounts

Money has a magical shrinking property, whereby the amount that is paid to you each year bears little resemblance to what eventually ends up in your pocket. Nevertheless, in an ideal world, instead of spending it all right away you will allocate some of your precious hard-earned cash into savings. The question then is where best to store it. Some people hide their money in the mattress or bury it underneath a favourite gnome, but putting it in a bank account is generally considered a better option.

A savings accounts pays you interest for keeping your money where it is for as long as possible. There are several different types of savings accounts, ranging from instant access through to accounts that require several months' notice before you can withdraw money. They should all pay a higher rate of interest than a current account, although interest rates range vastly depending on the individual bank or building society's rates.

Instant access accounts are the most straightforward form of savings account. They offer the possibility of simple, small-scale saving and immediate access to your money if necessary. You can open one online or by going into a building society, bank or credit union.

Regular savings accounts and notice accounts work like instant access accounts but you can earn more interest by committing to regular payments and keeping your money stashed away for longer. Both of these types of accounts are good for putting money away for a longer period of time, enabling yourself to save for longer-term goals such as a holiday or decorating your home.

A notice account requires advance, written notice if you want to withdraw your money. You can choose your notice period, ranging from 30-90 days; the longer the notice period, the higher the interest rate.

Bonds are savings accounts that tie up your money for several years at a time, but also earn better interest rates than other types of accounts. You can choose to have the interest paid out to you as you go along, while not touching the original amount which is left alone to keep earning interest. Some bonds are stock-market linked so the interest may vary. You can open a bond at your bank or through a financial adviser.

→ **www.moneyfacts.co.uk** – This is an independent company that newspapers and financial experts use to compare different savings accounts.

ISAs (Individual Savings Accounts) have been introduced by the government to encourage people to save. They allow you to accrue interest without paying any Income or Capital Gains tax on it. Each tax year – which runs from April 6 to April 5 – anyone who pays tax is allowed to save up to a remarkable maximum of £7,200 into an ISA.

ISAs divide your savings into either cash, or stocks and shares. You can put in up to £3,600 of that in cash. If you want to put in your full allowance the remainder will have to be in shares. Alternatively, you can invest the entire amount in shares. **ISAs are not actual investments, they are more like wrappers that protect your interest from tax.**

You can open an ISA through a bank or building society, or through a financial adviser. Share ISAs are more risky than cash ISAs, therefore it's always a good idea to get specialist advice if you would like to open one (see **Professional Advice** chapter).

→ **www.hmrc.gov.uk/leaflets/isa-factsheet.htm** – The government's fact sheet for more essential information.

→ **www.direct.gov.uk** – Find here up-to-date specifications on ISA allowances.

Interest

You can compare different types of accounts and the interest they offer by using the AER, which stands for Annual Equivalent Rate. The AER shows what the rate would be if the interest were paid annually instead of monthly or quarterly. It allows you to work out how much each account would cost you – or earn you – over a year.

If you can resist temptation and leave your money in a savings account for long enough your interest will start to earn interest too – this is known as compound interest, and is a great exhilarating factor for your nest egg.

Tax

If you are a taxpayer the interest on your savings also gets taxed – this happens at source, which means that you don't really notice it and you don't have to take any action. The only exception is, of course, the funds you keep in your ISA.

Inflation

Inflation can mean that anything you save today will be worth a lot less in the future. For example, twenty years ago, savings of £100 would have bought you a great deal more than the same amount would today. To beat inflation, you will need to review how much you save on a regular basis. **If your savings don't attract at least as much interest as the going rate of inflation you actually lose money.** Which is, by the way, a great argument to abandon the money-under-the-mattress technique and get friendly with a savings account.

→ **www.bankofengland.co.uk** – Check out the current rate of inflation here.

Sharia products

Sharia products are those which adhere to the five 'pillars' of an Islamic society: faith, life, wealth, intellect and posterity. Islamic law forbids paying or receiving interest but allows trading. This leads to interesting twists where banks, for example, buy a house (the house you like) and sell it to you for a higher price and let you pay in installments. Also known as mortgage, but with the cunning difference that namely no interest is involved.

With a Sharia bank account your money will not be invested in or deal with companies involved in pork products, alcohol, tobacco, gambling, armaments and pornography. Nowadays all banks have Islamic banking departments and there is also an index – the Global Islamic Index – which lists the performance of all companies complying with Sharia law.

→ **www.islamic-banking.com** – The Institute of Islamic Banking and Insurance can supply more specific information.

Ethical Banking

You don't have to be a superhero to save the world. Which is lucky, because while the muscle-hugging lycra might go down a treat in certain nightclubs, people might start to stare when you go down to the shops.

Ethical banking is one way to achieve a warm inner glow without eating a vindaloo. Once you start looking, a lot of investments – sooner or later – can be traced back to something unpleasant. By banking ethically, you can make your mark by choosing not to invest in companies connected with things you disapprove of and still make your money work for you.

The power to make a difference
In 1959 a small group of people gathered in London to protest about the apartheid regime in South Africa. As awareness grew, people throughout the UK started to find out about the human rights abuses and widespread outrage gathered force from the 1960s onwards. Initially, shoppers stopped buying South African produce – such as fruit and cigarettes – and tourists stopped booking holidays there. Then people started to realize that they could hit where it hurt – at the finances that kept the regime going.

The UK banks that did business with the apartheid regime were targeted. People stopped opening accounts with them and those who already had accounts with them left in their thousands. This led directly to the birth of ethical investing – also known as 'socially responsible investing'. It wasn't led by big business, it was led by individuals who closed their current accounts and wrote letters to the banks explaining why they were doing so. The pioneers who started by warning shoppers against buying Cape-grown apples led the way to a financial revolution. Since then, investors have been using their collective bargaining power to make sure companies adopt human rights policies or codes of good business conduct.

Ethical banks

The best-known ethical bank in the UK is the Co-operative Bank, which has been around since the nineteenth century. Since the 1970s it has made a conscious effort to be responsible – originally offering free banking to any customers who didn't get into debt (a far cry from the other banks who actively encouraged their customers to do so). The Co-op now refuses to invest in companies involved in activities such as animal testing, arms dealing and genetic modification, and actively supports institutions involved in green activities, such as recycling, reducing carbon emissions and fair trade. There's also an online branch of the Co-op called Smile.

→ **www.co-operativebank.co.uk**
→ **www.smile.co.uk**

Other ethical banks include:

The Triodos Bank, which only lends to businesses involved in sustainable development projects such as solar and wind energy.

→ **www.triodos.co.uk**

The Ecology Building Society specializes in mortgages for energy-efficient housing, ecological renovation, derelict and dilapidated properties and small-scale and ecological enterprise.

→ **www.ecologybuildingsociety.co.uk**

The Charity Bank was set up in 2002 and is the UK's first registered charity which is also a bank. Like a bank, it is regulated by the Financial Services Authority.

→ **www.charitybank.org**

Professional Advice

Gone are the days when financial advice meant discussing pensions over tea and biscuits with your bank manager, signing a couple of forms and promptly forgetting about the whole business. Friendly bank managers, like those sketchy-looking salesmen who used to turn up on the front doorstep offering you a good deal on life insurance, are now few and far between.

When it comes to major financial decisions you really want to speak to a financial adviser. They, as almost everything connected to finance, come in a variety of shapes and sizes. A financial adviser should be able to hook you up with whatever it is you desire, be it a pension or Alien abduction insurance – and yes, the latter does exist.

When Do You Need Financial Advice?

There are certain products you can only buy through specialist advisers, for example shares can only be bought through a stockbroker – but a stockbroker won't always be able to advise you on what shares to buy. That's when you need to seek out independent advice.

You might also want an adviser to see you through the financial forests that surround mortgages and life insurance. Both are things you can buy yourself, but you may not want to choose without knowing all the facts. Some companies give special deals if you buy through a financial adviser, meaning it shouldn't end up costing you anything to do so.

A good financial adviser will know all the latest financial products and make sure you get the best possible deal for your money. They will also ensure that you get the most suitable investment or product. If you have been mis-sold a product in the past, a financial adviser may even be able to help you claim compensation.

There are thousands of websites that want to advise you on financial matters. Some try to sell you their own products and some will give independent advice. Here is a selection of a few that we can recommend:

→ **www.moneymadeclear.fsa.gov.uk** – The Financial Services Authority (FSA) is the government-appointed organization that regulates the sale of financial products such as mortgages and insurance. Here, you'll find advice on financial products as well as useful guides on all things money-related.

→ **www.unbiased.co.uk** – Find an independent financial adviser in your area here.

→ **www.step.org** – The Society of Trust & Estate Practitioners (STEP) list local inheritance tax experts.

→ **www.londonstockexchange.co.uk** – In the London Stock Exchange site search bar, type 'find a broker' and you can choose from a list of brokers in your area.

→ **www.financial-ombudsman.org.uk** – The Financial Ombudsman Service handles complaints regarding financial products.

Choosing A Financial Adviser

There are many different types of financial adviser, some work independently, some are affiliated to particular companies. Some charge you a fee, those that don't will be getting paid a commission from the companies whose financial products you buy. Advisers and the companies they work for have to be registered with the FSA; if you are unsure about anything you are being offered you can go online and check the status of your financial adviser through the FSA's website.

You can shop around for financial advisers using resources such as online comparison sites, the financial pages of newspapers and specialist consumer magazines including *Which?*, *What Mortgage* or *What Investment* to see what's available so you have a working knowledge of the subject and won't be blinded by financial science when you meet your adviser.

Here is a neat overview of the different species of advisers you might come across:

Independent advisers, also known as IFAs or financial planners, are not affiliated to any particular company and have access to every product available. They are qualified to sell mortgages, life insurance and pensions. When you first see an adviser they will print out a Keyfacts document as well as an Initial Disclosure Document; this will prove that they are independent and detail how they get paid.

Multi-tied advisers are advisers who may have arrangements with several different providers or companies. This means they should be able to offer a choice, but they won't be able to source all of the possible deals available, only those through the companies they work with.

Tied advisers are simply advisers that sell the products of only one company. For example, if you go to your bank and ask about a mortgage, the chances are the adviser you speak to will only be able to sell you mortgages offered by that particular bank.

Financial planners are fee-based advisers who will give you holistic financial advice, like going to the hairdresser for a cut and blowdry and being offered reflexology at the same time. For example, they may help you budget as well as invest your money.

Stockbrokers are authorized to sell shares, as are some financial advisers. Many stockbrokers aren't authorized to give advice, which means that you have to decide what shares you want to buy and then pay the stockbroker to buy them for you.

Accountants will normally advise you on tax, but some are also trained financial advisers and some also work as stockbrokers.

Saving for Emergencies

Smug people will often tell you that life is a rollercoaster – but you wouldn't hop onto a rollercoaster without a secure safety harness, would you?

An existence of average length will fling all kinds of setbacks and challenges your way. An unexpected expense, illness or finding yourself unemployed can throw you financially off-kilter.

There may also be unmissable opportunities that you need a bit of spare cash to take advantage of. For occasions such as these, emergency savings are a useful fallback. If, at any time, you find yourself with any money to set aside, it's worth maintaining a safety fund.

Why Have a Safety Net?

The words 'saving' and 'emergencies' don't normally go hand in hand, but cash flow problems can affect everyone – individuals, companies, banks and sometimes even whole countries. Having an emergency fund can help ease you out of those tricky situations, but will mainly provide you with great peace of mind.

How Much Should It Be?

How much you will need in your emergency pot is dependent on your lifestyle. If, for instance, you live in an old house that's likely to need sudden repairs, are firmly wedded to an ancient MG that wants constant servicing, or have a family to take care of, all these things need to be taken into consideration. The more responsibilities you have, the bigger your emergency pot should be (see **The Next Generation** chapter).

A good figure to aim for is having at least three months' worth of expenses in a savings account. That means enough to cover three months of mortgage/rent, bills, any debt repayments, those direct debits you often forget about such as mobile phone, insurance and credit-card payments, and essentials such as food, train fares and the odd trip to the pub. If you then have to give up work for a while all the basics will be covered.

If you are self-employed, aiming for six months' worth of expenses is ideal; this should be enough to help you through most financial headaches.

Emergency funds need to be reviewed every six or twelve months. Your savings should be up to date with your lifestyle, so you avoid a huge drop in comfort should you have to rely on it.

Where Should It Live?

As with all kinds of savings it makes sense to squirrel away the amount you want to save bit by bit. The least painful is probably to set up a direct debit and dedicate a percentage of your monthly income to a special account. The emergency pot should be in an account that carries a low risk (i.e. it shouldn't be invested in shares, for example) and is instantly accessible should you need it.

Unlike other kinds of savings, the emergency fund isn't about getting the highest interest. An instant access account, or one with only a small notice period, will let you get at your emergency cash in a hurry. It's not a good idea to use your ISA in this way, if you can help it. Unlike savings accounts, ISAs only let you put a certain amount into them per year and don't allow you to replace any money taken out.

Credit card for emergencies

Should you have to use money locked away in an account with a notice period for an emergency, it can be handy to bridge the notice time with funds from a credit card. Generally, if you are self employed, or just starting work, having a credit card with a small balance can be a useful stop gap. But this is only advisable for the disciplined who pay their credit-card bills every month.

Insurance

Life's great, but it can have its bleaker moments. For such occasions you have insurance. You can insure just about anything, from your lifeblood to a tricycle, and in exchange for regular payments, you can rest assured that if the worst happens, there will at least be some sort of a payout.

Income Protection Insurance

Income protection insurance guarantees to pay a monthly income if you can't work due to redundancy or illness, and thus can be a great emergency-relief investment. Income protection is not intended to make you better off than you were before you got ill, so big payouts are uncommon. It should pay out enough to cover the essentials such as credit-card, loan and mortgage payments, and basics like phone and electricity bills. Self-employed people will really need to shop around as not all policies are suitable for them.

If you can't afford income protection, a cheaper option is to take out accident, sickness and unemployment cover. Unlike income protection, it will only pay out for a limited period, normally two years, whereas – in the event of a permanently disabling condition – many income protection policies pay out indefinitely.

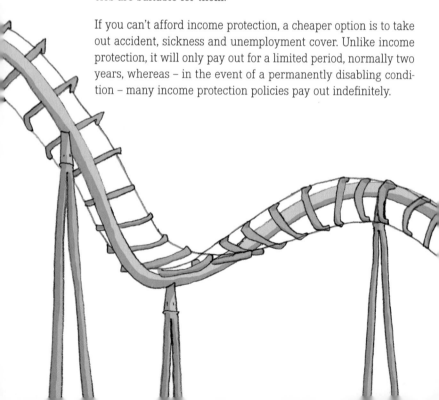

Pet insurance

Our little four-legged friends can sometimes rack up quite a bar tab at the vet, and there's not always money left over in the monthly pot for an emergency surgery or illness. Pet insurance will pay towards vet's bills and any drugs your pet needs as well as the cost of helping to find a pet that has been lost. As vet's bills are crazily high, this really can save you some serious money in the long run.

Mortgages

It's probably the most expensive thing you'll ever own, but **buying a home is the best investment you're likely to make**, not to mention the opportunity to live out the dreams of a thousand home improvement shows. There are few things more important than having a roof over your head. For most people – barring those who've won the lottery – buying a home involves having to take out a mortgage.

Along with bereavement and marriage, buying a house is supposed to be among the most stressful times of your life, but it's worth persevering with.

Mortgage Basics

Most mortgages run for 25 years, but there are some lenders who'll allow you to repay your mortgage over a longer term, as much as 40 years. Some mortgages also come with an option to overpay, which means you make larger payments when you can afford them and therefore end up clearing your mortgage sooner. **Paying off a mortgage early is a smart move as you'll be saving yourself thousands of pounds in interest.**

A mortgage is a secured loan; what this means is that the company (normally a bank or building society) lending the money will own part of the property – as security – until the mortgage has been paid off. This means that if repayments aren't kept up, the property can be sold by the mortgage lender in order to pay off the loan.

Applying for a mortgage can be a lengthy and frustrating process involving appointing a solicitor and a surveyor and – the hardest bit – being prepared to wait for at least three months for everything to go through.

The amount you can borrow

What people can afford to borrow depends on how much they earn and how much they can afford to repay each month. In rare circumstances some lenders will agree to a 100% mortgage, which doesn't require the borrower providing a deposit up front. It is, however, much more usual to be required to pay a deposit (see opposite).

If you are buying your first home most lenders will, at the moment, allow you to borrow an amount worth three-and-a-half times your annual salary; if you are buying with a partner or friend you can normally borrow two and a half times your joint salary. If you are on the way up the property ladder, lenders will tend to allow you to borrow more; for example if your home has increased in value you'll have built up what lenders call 'equity', which you can then use to remortgage.

A good mortgage adviser will be able to do an affordability check; this works out exactly how much someone should be borrowing by taking into account such things as salary, outgoings, possible bonuses and debts. It then comes up with what kind of mortgage would be suitable.

The deposit

A deposit is the amount of money paid up front. For instance, if you want to buy a property worth £200,000 and you have £15,000 for a deposit, you will need a mortgage of £185,000. The larger the deposit, the cheaper the mortgage will be. Lenders will usually suggest a deposit should be a minimum of 5% of the property price.

You don't have to have a mortgage in place before you find a potential home, but it can speed things up. If you prefer, before you start house hunting you can ask the mortgage lender for what's known as an agreement in principle; it means the lender has checked you out and given you a provisional mortgage offer. An agreement in principle shows estate agents and vendors that you're not wasting their time.

Valuation and survey

Once you've found your dream pad, you need to secure it by making an offer. If the offer is accepted the mortgage lender will then insist on a valuation to make sure the property is worth the offered price.

The valuation will be carried out by a qualified surveyor. There are several different types of valuation; all have to include important information that could alter the property's value in the near future – for example, if it has damp or subsidence. If the valuation comes back with a number of problems – and most do – it will be expected that as long as the buyer still wants the property they will make a lower offer. This means that the money saved on the purchase can go towards repairing the problems. If the valuation comes up with no problems, then hopefully the offer should go through without a hitch.

Choosing the Right Kind of Mortgage

There were, at last count, around 20,000 different types of mortgage available. Whoah! To narrow things down a bit, you need to consider how you want to pay back your mortgage.

Mortgages come in two types: *interest only* and *repayment*.

Everyone with a mortgage pays interest, that's how the banks earn their money, but how you pay the major part of your loan – what's known as the 'capital part' – will depend on whether you choose a repayment or interest-only mortgage.

If you borrow £200,000 with a repayment mortgage, what you'll be paying is the £200,000 plus the interest. This means that your monthly payments will pay off the total amount of the loan as you go along. If you take out an interest-only mortgage, however, you will just pay off the interest, leaving you with £200,000 still to pay at the end of the mortgage term. If you have an interest-only mortgage, your monthly repayments will be lower, because you are not paying off all of the loan.

If you decide to take out an interest-only mortgage, the repayments may be cheaper but you'll need to take out another savings product, like an Individual Savings Account (ISA), in order to save up enough to pay off the rest when the time comes.

Interest calculation

Once you've decided how you want to repay your mortgage, now you need to choose how to pay your interest. There are two main ways you can do so: on a variable basis, where your repayments will change according to the base rate; or on a fixed basis, where you can set your repayments for a defined amount of time.

An easy way to work out interest is by doubling the amount you originally borrow and realizing that as the figure you will finally repay. Advisers who specialize in mortgages reckon this is a good rule of thumb to follow, because on a mortgage you tend to end up paying as much interest as the original loan.

For example, if you borrow £100,000 and your mortgage charges 5% interest, what you'll end up paying is 5% of £100,000 each year that you have the mortgage. So on a loan of £100,000 you'll pay around £5,000 per year in interest, plus around £4,000 a year of the original amount you owe. That's a total of £9,000 a year or around £750 a month.

Fixed-rate interest

This is a popular way of making sure your repayments stay the same regardless of what happens to the base rate. You can choose to fix the amount of interest you'll pay for several years; this could range from two to more than 10 years. This can be a great deal. The only problem is that, if you decide you want to swap your mortgage (see re-mortgaging later on) before your fixed rate deal ends, you'll normally have to pay a redemption or penalty charge. That's because, in order to allow you to borrow at a set rate, banks will have to pay extra to borrow the money at a set rate themselves.

If interest rates fall below your set fixed-interest rate, you'll be the chump paying more than average. Alternatively, if they rise above, you can smile smugly to yourself because you are saving more money than those other losers paying back their mortgages with variable-rate interest.

Variable-rate interest

Quite simply, your interest rate is likely to change if the Bank of England's base rate changes. Lenders will have their own base rate, known as the lender's standard variable rate. This rate will normally be slightly above the Bank of England's base rate. This is very good news when the base rate goes down; not good news when the base rate goes up. It's worth mentioning that rates are very quick to increase, yet can take several months to decrease and it is at the lenders' discretion whether they reduce at all.

The Base Rate Explained

The Bank of England's Monetary Policy Committee, known as the MPC, is a group of economists appointed by the government. Every month this group sits down to debate what to do with the bank's base rate. The base rate will determine what lenders, such as banks and building societies, will have to pay when they themselves want to borrow money. This in turn determines how much those institutions need to charge the people borrowing from them – this is the interest rate and it varies from lender to lender.

The interest rate is what will make someone with a mortgage sit up when the financial news comes on: a higher interest rate means higher mortgage repayments and a lower rate means reduced monthly payments. The MPC will raise interest rates at times when the group feels it should be encouraging people to save money – this will normally be when consumer spending is too high. The rate is likely to be lowered if the MPC thinks the economy needs a boost.

Types of Mortgages

To give you a better idea of the variety of mortgages that are around, here is a short introduction to some of the species:

Trackers work in a similar way to variable-rate mortgages. The difference is that the mortgage tracks the Bank of England base rate instead of the lender's variable rate. The benefit is that you are guaranteed to benefit from the full effect of any rate cut, rather than whether your lender decides to reduce their standard variable rate.

Discounted mortgages are based on the lender's standard variable rate but will discount between 1% and 2% below this. Discounted rates tend only to be offered for fixed-rate periods – between two and three years – and like standard variable-rate mortgages, repayments can go up as well as down.

Flexible mortgages are mortgages that allow you to overpay and underpay, or even take repayment holidays (see box below). Some will allow you to offset any savings you have against your mortgage interest rate, so you can choose to lower your mortgage interest payments by paying less on your savings.

The proviso with most flexible mortgages is that you agree to pay in a minimum amount each year, and once you've made those payments you can choose to underpay. There are limits on what you can overpay and underpay each year. A lot of people use flexible mortgages to pay off a mortgage early because they don't have such strict redemption penalties as a standard mortgage.

On the other hand, most non-flexible schemes allow over-payment as well – some up to 10% or 20% per year – and often have lower interest rates than true flexible schemes.

Guarantor mortgages can be used when someone wants to borrow more than the standard three-and-a-half times annual salary multiple required by most mortgage lenders. This is when someone other than the main borrower – such as a parent or very close friend – agrees to be included on the mortgage agreement as a guarantor, or the person who will be responsible for making sure the mortgage is paid. Before approving a guarantor mortgage, the lender will take into account the guarantor's personal mortgage, loans and financial status in addition to those of the applicant.

APR

This is short for Annual Percentage Rate. The APR does include the interest rate you'll pay but it also takes into account other charges – for example, if you miss a mortgage payment or choose to pay your mortgage off early. The APR averages out the amount you'll pay each year and is a good way of comparing different mortgages.

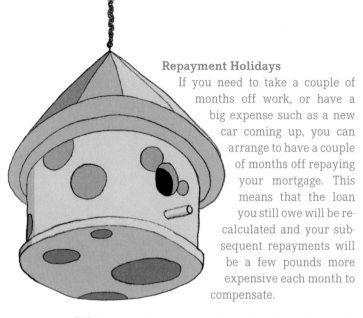

Repayment Holidays

If you need to take a couple of months off work, or have a big expense such as a new car coming up, you can arrange to have a couple of months off repaying your mortgage. This means that the loan you still owe will be re-calculated and your subsequent repayments will be a few pounds more expensive each month to compensate.

Lifetime mortgages are a form of equity release and are sold through independent financial advisers. Lifetime mortgages are only available to older applicants, the minimum age being 55-60 years old. The older you are, the more equity can be released. They allow homeowners to use the value of their home as a way of raising extra cash, normally after they have retired. A lifetime mortgage does mean that the bank will own part of your home but there are strict guidelines as to how these mortgages are sold.

Buy-to-let mortgages are the same as normal mortgages except the amount you can borrow will depend on how much rental income you are expected to get. Nearly all buy-to-let mortgages will require a deposit, as the most lenders will allow you to borrow is 85 per cent of the property price. Lenders might also let you use your income and add the rental income to your salary, while others base the loan entirely on rent.

Buy-to-let mortgages can be more expensive than most mortgages and there is no direct tax relief on them, but you can offset interest payments on your mortgage against the tax on your rental income, along with other expenses such as agents' fees and maintenance costs.

Self-certification – If someone is self-employed the usual salary criteria will not apply; this is because the income of someone who works for themselves goes up and down from year to year. Some lenders will allow borrowers to estimate – using their latest tax return – how much they expect to earn in the next financial year. Most lenders will expect any estimates to be backed up with some kind of written confirmation from a chartered accountant. There are a number of lenders that specialize in mortgages for the self-employed.

Sub-prime mortgages – If someone has in the past got into financial difficulty, such as a missed loan payment or a county court judgement, they will still be able to take out a mortgage, but they will have to pay a slightly higher rate of interest because they are considered to be more risky. There are various levels of what are known as 'sub-prime' mortgages, varying from a 'near prime', which might be only slightly more expensive than a standard mortgage, to an 'unlimited sub-prime' where the rate may be two per cent higher than the lender's standard rate. Someone who has been made bankrupt would normally have to take out a heavier version of a sub-prime mortgage.

Getting that mortgage offer

If you are interested in a particular mortgage you can ask for a keyfacts document. This will have all the important mortgage information you need to know and can help you to compare the one you are considering with other mortgages, to see which offers you the best deal. When you've decided on a particular mortgage you will get a similar document known as a keyfacts illustration or KFI. This is a more detailed version and will include more specific information relating to your own circumstances.

Other Mortgage Terms

Here are some explanations of the mortgage jargon that you're sure to come across when you start looking to buy a house:

Loan to value – This often appears in paperwork as the 'LTV' and describes the amount you are borrowing in comparison to how much the property is worth. A 100 per cent LTV means you are borrowing the full amount of the property's value, i.e. putting down no deposit. An 85 per cent LTV mortgage means the borrower is putting down a 15 per cent deposit.

Higher lending charge or mortgage indemnity guarantee – If you don't have a deposit to put down the lender may charge you for the plain fact that they are having to cover the entire cost of the property. Not all lenders will charge this.

Remortgaging – If you already own a home with a mortgage, you don't have to stick with your original mortgage lender forever. You can decide to go to another company and 'remortgage'. This means that you are replacing your existing mortgage with another one. People remortgage in order to get a better deal with a new company, sometimes they do it to raise money by taking out a higher mortgage, or simply to raise extra cash for home improvements or investment. It might also be a good thing to do when a fixed-rate deal comes to an end. The costs of remortgaging might, however, put you off as you may have to pay expenses including solicitor's fees, valuation fees and possibly an early redemption penalty.

Early redemption charges – These are the charges you pay if you pay a mortgage off early, and are charged to cover the cost of the lender's lost interest payments. A redemption penalty can be charged as a percentage of the loan you originally took out or they can be charged at a cost of several months' worth of interest. If you believe there's a chance you may be able to pay your loan off early then check with your lender before agreeing to the mortgage as not all lenders charge this fee.

Deeds release fee – If you decide to remortgage, you may have to pay a deeds release fee – usually a charge of around £300 – in order to cover the costs of moving from one company to another.

Conveyancer – This is the name given to a solicitor who specializes in property purchases. The conveyancer is responsible for drawing up all contracts, and the deeds, in order to finalize the purchase of your new home.

Home Information Packs (HIP) – When you are considering buying a house, the seller is obliged to give you a HIP detailing vital information about the property, thereby allowing you to make a more informed decision about purchasing. A HIP is provided to potential buyers free of charge. Amongst other things, it has to include an Energy Performance Certificate (EPC), which will tell you how energy-efficient the home is, as well as contain advice on how to cut carbon emissions and fuel bills.

Stamp duty – Stamp duty is a special tax that applies if you are buying a property that costs over £125,000 (although in a very few disadvantaged areas of the UK the stamp duty threshold doesn't start until £150,001). If you buy a property worth between £125,000 and £200,000 you will have to pay a tax worth 1% of its value. For a property worth between £250,001 and £500,000 you will have to pay 3% of its value and for properties £500,001 and over, the stamp duty rises to 4%.

And finally...

Exchange of contract – This is the point when you are legally bound to buy the property, exchanging contracts with the person who is selling you the property. If the sale falls through after the exchange of contract you may be expected to pay a deposit of 10 per cent of the property's value.

Completion – This follows the exchange of contracts and is when the keys of your new home are safely in your pocket.

Protect Your Home

Now that you've got the mortgage, it's important to consider the ways in which you can **minimize the risk of losing the home in which you're investing**. Imagine working to save up a deposit for a mortgage, and then some terrible disaster happens, such as the house burning down, and you still have to keep paying the mortgage even though there's no porch left. Or roof. Or walls. You get the idea. In order to guard against the tragedy of this possibility, you need housing insurance. Onwards!

Buildings insurance

This pays the cost of repairing or rebuilding your home if it is damaged by what insurers refer to as 'an unforeseen event'. When you buy a house you will be required to take out buildings cover, but what this covers will depend on the individual policy. Some policies will pay out only in extreme circumstances, such as if your home is damaged by flood or fire, whereas others pay for all buildings damage, such as broken windows.

Contents insurance

Buildings insurance does not cover the cost of replacing your possessions, so for that you'll need to take out contents insurance.

It covers items in your home that are stolen or damaged. You can tailor what kind of cover you want – specifying, for example, if you want it to cover precious music equipment, a mountain bike or an expensive laptop. Most policies tend to cover you against fire and theft, but you can also insure against accidental damage – for instance, if someone drops your camera onto your brand new, and very hard, kitchen floor. Some policies will also insure your possessions if you take them abroad – check when buying the policy.

Mortgage Payment Protection Insurance (MPPI)

This is also known as accident, sickness and unemployment insurance. A typical policy is designed to begin covering your mortgage payments one month after your income stops due to redundancy, accident or illness, and continue for 12 months (see **Saving for Emergencies** chapter). This type of insurance is often not great for self-employed people, as it's hard to prove exactly when your employment stopped, so you'll need to shop around for the insurance policies created specifically for the self-employed.

~~Pensions~~ Endless Pleasures

Pensions are an effective way to save for your retirement for many reasons, not least that they offer some fine opportunities for tax breaks. If you start investing in a pension now, you shouldn't have to worry about spending mornings when in your 70s desperately collecting supermarket coupons for the weekly shop; instead you can spend your time relaxing and enjoying the freedom from work.

The difficulty is that when you are young, there are few things less sexy than thinking about retirement. Even more of a mood killer is thinking about how you are going to financially survive it. The sheer sound of the word 'pension' conjures up images of fake teeth, canes and coupons. Wouldn't it feel much easier spending 50 quid a month on something called 'endless pleasures' rather than putting the same amount towards 'a pension'? It might be time for a spot of re-branding.

Types of Pensions

There are three kinds of pensions: state, company, and private pensions. The government wants to encourage us to save as much as possible so all contributions to pensions are tax free. When you finally collect your pension you won't pay capital gains tax either, although you may have to pay income tax on the money you get.

State pensions

Every month, when you pay your National Insurance (NI) contributions, you are basically paying for the state pension of the sweet old lady next door. At the moment, the state retirement age is 65, but the chances are that this will go up. When you reach retirement age you will hopefully be eligible for money from the NI contributions of the kid next door.

The problem is, with people living longer, healthier lives, and fewer children born per family, there is a smaller generation of youth paying for a much greater pool of healthy elderly. The government will have less money to put aside and this means that you need to start looking for ways to secure your retirement income today, not a few years shy of retirement, which means the endless pleasures of your winter years are in the hands of your financial intelligence in the here and now.

Basic State Pension (BSP)

This is the pension paid out to anyone who has paid National Insurance. If you've worked 30 years or more full-time, chances are you will get the full rate. If you haven't worked for a full 30 years, then you'll get a percentage of this rate. At the moment, the full basic State Pension is around £87 a week for a single person and £140 a week for a couple, but this amount varies depending on the circumstance. Couples receive less because they can share basic utility costs between them, like heating and electricity. No one knows for sure how much the BSP will be when you reach retirement age, but even if it were as much as today, you clearly need to have some substantial savings or an additional pension to help you out with this belt-tightening budget.

Pension credit

Pension Credit is a state benefit paid out to 60 year olds who don't otherwise have enough to live on. It's also paid out as a reward to over 65s who have some savings. It basically tops up your income so that no pensioner will have to live on anything less than £124 a week.

State Second Pension (S2P)

Finally, there's the State Second Pension, yet another safety net system for receiving state funds. It functions as a top-up pension for people who are low-rate pensioners and in the lower-income bracket. It is a way to even out the score and be fair to those who have been unable to pay enough taxes in the past to accrue the full amount of Basic State Pension, perhaps due to disability, low income, long periods of illness or because they've been caring for someone else and therefore not able to work. Unfortunately, the self-employed are not entitled to S2P.

For more information, go to:

→ **www.direct.gov.uk/en/MoneyTaxAndBenefits/** – This comprehensive government site makes pensions surprisingly easy to digest. Choose the 'Pensions and Retirement' section to find out more about state pensions. You'll also find a link here to a state pension forecast which will calculate how much money you might have coming your way when it's time to collect.

www.thepensionservice.gov.uk – Everything you'll need to know about pensions, benefits, and how to plan for retirement.

You thought your student budget was tight, and that was only for around three years. Imagine living on a budget like the ones shown above for around 25 years! If an endless future of ramen and cutting corners and coupons isn't all that appealing to you, then you'll find the call of company and personal pensions pretty attractive.

Private Pensions

Private pensions include company, personal, stakeholder, and Self-Invested Personal Pensions (SIPPs). A private pension either comes with your job or you can buy it from a pension provider through banks or a life office. You can contribute to a private pension if you are employed, self-employed, or even unemployed.

Company pensions

People in employment might find that the firm they work for offers a company pension. This is a great method of saving for retirement, because while money is automatically deducted from the salary to pay into a pension, the employer will usually make a contribution to your pension as well, which works out like a pay-rise. Some company pension schemes don't even ask you to pay in, which means all your pension is paid for by your company.

There are two types of company pension schemes: defined contribution or defined benefit. The pay-outs of a defined contribution scheme (also known as money-purchase scheme) are based upon what you put into the fund and how well the investments perform, whereas the pay-outs of a defined benefit scheme are based upon how long you've worked and what you earn when you retire.

You can choose to top up your company pension scheme by investing in an additional voluntary contribution (AVC). These tend to be more expensive to set up than a normal pension but offer a good way to make up lost pension years if you started paying into your pension late or had to take a break.

Company pensions sometimes also offer other benefits such as life insurance or a pension pay-out to your family after you die. If your company doesn't offer a pension scheme, or if you are self-employed, it's definitely time to start looking into private pension schemes.

Money-purchase scheme

The expression 'money-purchase scheme' is one of those terms that people in love with calculators like to make up. It simply describes a scheme where the size of the eventual pot depends on how much money is put in and what the investment performance is over the term.

With all money-purchase arrangements, the dangers obviously lie in the risk. If the wrong investment decisions are made, then the money in the pension and the years of investment may be lost, and neither the government nor anyone else is liable to help pad out the fall.

Personal pensions

In addition to the state and company pensions, some people choose to boost their retirement income via a personal pension. This is a private, money-purchase pension, which means that it is not linked to salary and the investor chooses exactly when and how to contribute. Having a personal pension ultimately means you can retire earlier, because at the moment you are able to get ahold of your pension and buy round the world cruise tickets at 55 years old. Before then, you can decide to sell the assets of your private pension whenever you want as long as you have the money transferred to another pension scheme. Once you reach retirement age, you can withdraw up to 25% of your pension fund as a tax-free lump sum, which could for example be used to pay off a mortgage.

If and when you choose to take 25% of your pension fund lump sum, you can use the remaining 75% to make sure you have an income for the rest of your life, no matter how long you live. You do this by buying an annuity from an insurance company or annuity provider. You don't have to buy your annuity from your pension company, you can shop around, because like most other things the cost of an annuity can vary widely.

When you start paying into a pension your contributions will need to get bigger every year to take account of inflation, and to keep you up-to-date; your pension company will normally tell you how much you need to pay to keep up.

The beauty of personal pensions is that they offer the widest variety of investment options at a low cost. This is the type of pension you would need to invest in if you are self-employed.

With all pensions you can put in 100 per cent of your salary, up to a maximum of £225,000 a year. And if your total pension fund tops £1.5m, this is the Lifetime Allowance, then you have to pay a 55 per cent tax on any extra money above that.

Self-Invested Personal Pensions (SIPPs)

SIPPs are a kind of personal pension designed for people with large funds, who already know their way around the stock market. They are personal pensions with more room for investment. They come in two types: a basic version, which allows you to choose shares and funds, and a full version, which can also allow some types of property investment.

It's a lottery

Are you a lottery junkie? Money used to pay into a lottery ticket a few times a week could be much better spent on a pension. After all, week after week, a useless losing lottery ticket will reap you nothing but frustration and disappointment. However, if you're sixty-five and have no pension, we suggest that you start playing the lottery immediately.

Stakeholder pensions

Stakeholder pensions are money-purchase pensions, which means that they are not linked to your salary. How well they perform will depend on the expertise of the company investing your money. It's a pension that was designed for smaller companies with employees of five or more. **Any employer with more than five staff has to offer their staff access to a stakeholder scheme**, although they don't have to match your contributions.

The stakeholder options are more flexible in terms of contributions: you can make lump-sum or regular contributions, and the minimum required contributions are lower than any other personal pensions – as low as £20 per week, month, or less regularly. And as with most other private pensions, you can also choose to stop payments on your pension and restart later without accruing any penalty fees.

→ **www.pensionsorter.co.uk/savingscalculator.cfm** – This pension calculator is a one-two punch calculator that shows you how £50 a month under the mattress for 45 years can be increased from £27,000 to £314,000 if you add it into a personal pension scheme instead.

The Next Generation

According to exam results, the nation's youth grow cleverer every year. If things continue at this rate, perhaps we can look forward to a bright future in which, from the moment of their entry into the world, our children are financial geniuses, rocking around in wifi-enabled prams, keeping one beady eye on SpongeBob and the other on the Dow Jones Index.

Until this happy day, however, you may have to look after your children's funds, at least through their formative years. Handily, there are structures in place to help you do this, so the whole business isn't the pea-souper you might expect.

Child Trust Funds

Child Trust Funds are a government-initiated saving and investment account for children. They are a tax-free way to kick-start kids' savings, like an ISA for beginners (see **Banking** chapter) – and you get free money to start them off. Every child born on or after 1 September 2002 will have had a Child Trust Fund account opened up for them by the lovely folks over at the Inland Revenue.

Child Trust Funds cannot be withdrawn until the youngster reaches eighteen, and from then on will attract tax on interest and capital gains. At the time of writing, in a gesture of blinding generosity, the government starts off the fund with a £250 voucher and then contributes a further £250 when the child turns seven. Families who qualify for full Child Tax Credit receive £500 at birth, and £500 at seven years of age.

→ **www.hmrc.gov.uk** – The Inland Revenue website, where you can discover what kind of CTF voucher your children will qualify for and to keep an eye on proposed changes to the system.

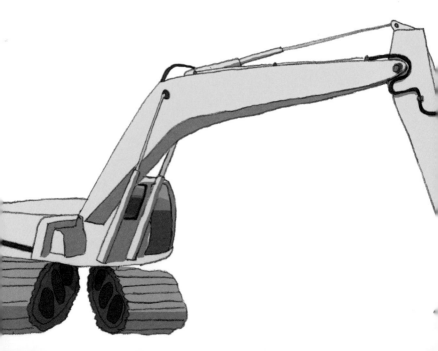

How to start your child's CTF

When a child is born, the parents will need to get in touch with the CTF people. A CTF voucher will then be posted out to them. If the CTF voucher is not transformed into an account by the parents within a year, the Inland Revenue automatically invests the cash into a stakeholder Child Trust Fund for that named child, so hopefully no child should miss out on the fund to which they're entitled.

→ **http://taxcredits.direct.gov.uk** – Information on eligibility and how to claim Child Tax Credits.

→ **www.childtrustfund.gov.uk** – Everything you need to know about whether you're entitled to and how to apply for a Child Trust Fund, as well as all the latest updates.

→ **www.dwp.gov.uk/lifeevent/benefits** – Information on benefits that you can claim if you have children.

Types of CTFs

There are three types of CTF: Cash, Stakeholder, and Equity. Parents, relatives and friends can add up to £1,200 per year into the fund, regardless of what type of CTF the child has. The children themselves can add to their individual funds later, too.

Cash CTF – If the voucher is put into a cash CTF you are basically opening an ordinary deposit savings account. Cash CTFs are the easiest CTF accounts to understand, but fewer of them are available than in the past. Only a few banks still offer cash CTFs, but you can find them easily enough at building societies.

Over the long term, **most investment experts agree that deposit accounts are outperformed by stock-market-based investments**. For example, over eighteen years a cash CTF will pay an interest rate of between 5 and 6 per cent. If this interest rate stays the same, the initial £250 voucher will only be worth around £600 by the time the child can get it, versus several thousand if invested in stock-based CTFs.

Stakeholder CTF – The money in these accounts is used to invest – albeit indirectly – in stocks and shares. Because they tend to be tracker accounts, which invest in a wide variety of different companies, they are considered less risky than investing directly in the stock market.

Assuming an average return of at least 6 per cent, and a £250 contribution at birth and again at the age of 7, the fund could grow to at least £1,188. **A £250 contribution at birth and at age 7 plus £1,200 each year can grow to over £40,000 by the time the child reaches 18.**

Equity CTF – Parents who are money savvy and are prepared to take a bit of a risk to get higher returns should consider an equity CTF, which invests directly in shares.

Equity CTFs are similar to stakeholder CTFs but they have the advantage of offering a wider range of investment. They are also more expensive as buying shares means dealing costs and an annual management charge, but obviously have the potential to perform very well.

→ **www.moneyfacts.co.uk** – Helps make sense of the different product options for all types of Child Trust Funds.

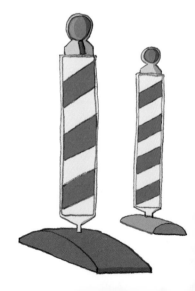

Life Insurance

If you have a family or other dependants, taking out life insurance is a really good way to provide yourself with peace of mind that they'll be taken care of after you've gone. Morbid, perhaps, but prudent.

There are two types of life insurance, one is known as 'whole-of-life' and the other as 'term'. The latter covers you for a set amount of time and for whatever you specify needs covering. It is the kind of life cover normally taken out with a mortgage and means you can make sure your home is paid for if you should die before the mortgage is paid off (see **Mortgage** chapter). This is especially important if you have dependants who could otherwise lose their home. It doesn't only apply to mortgages, it is also something that you might take out if, for example, you get married, you or your spouse gives birth, or your career takes on a more risky tack, such as becoming self-employed in which the safety net of employee benefits have been lost.

Not surprisingly, whole-of-life insurance lasts for your entire life – well, as long as you keep paying the premiums. You specify in the policy who you want the money to go to in the event of your death – your spouse, children, parents or your favourite poodle. The money that you pay in is usually invested in a stockmarket-linked fund, so the insurance company can make money on it before they need to pay out on your policy.

It is really an investment rather than an insurance policy – as the insurers are definitely going to have to pay out some day. Whole-of-life insurance is usually purchased from a specialist insurance adviser, rather than online. Non-investment linked whole-of-life policies are also widely available now in which the premium is fixed, but more expensive.

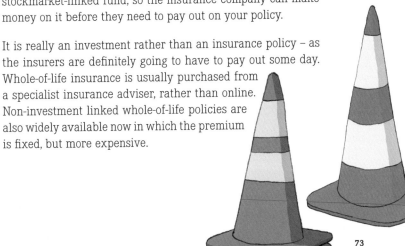

Inheritance Tax (IHT)

Chances are that at some point in your life, you will inherit something. That's when you need to know about inheritance tax.

Spouses that survive their partner should – unless the dead person's will says otherwise – inherit their partner's estate, and they won't have to pay any tax. If, however, you don't want to leave everything to your spouse – for example, if you have children or other family or friends you want some of your money to go to – the implications of inheritance tax are something to take into consideration.

In recent years property prices have risen much faster than the IHT tax limit, with the result that even one-bedroom flats in expensive areas now fall into the IHT tax bracket. This means that if you inherit your great aunt Ethel's tiny flat that cost £750 when she was a young bride, it may now be worth so much that paying the inheritance tax will be prohibitive – meaning **you will end up having to sell the property just in order to pay the tax**.

Any wealth you own above the allowed amount – which is currently £350,000 – including any proceeds gained from selling your house, will be taxed at 40 per cent when you die.

→ **www.step.org** – The Society of Trust & Estate Practitioners (STEP), the website lists local inheritance tax experts.

→ **www.unbiased.co.uk** – Find independent advice on all finances, from pensions to general investments.

The seven rule

The seven rule means that if you give away your wealth – for example, legally signing your property over to your children – at least seven years before you die, they don't have to pay inheritance tax on the gift. If, however, you die in less than seven years, the inheritance tax laws still apply.

Life lessons

Above all, the most important way you can help save for your family's next generation is to teach them how to save for themselves. It is truly one of the most valuable lessons a kid can learn, and one that too few ever do until it's too late and they're drowning in credit-card debt. The early introduction to saving will lead to a more prosperous financial future. The Jesuits said: 'Give me a child until he is seven and I will give you the man.'

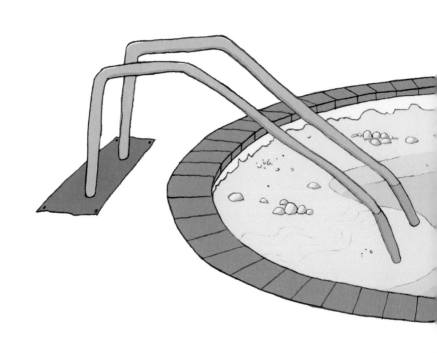

Time to Play

Once you've got a basic savings plan in place, **it's time to have some serious fun with your spare cash**. You can finally work towards satisfying your more ambitious desires. If you're a dedicated treasure hunter, sooner or later you'll need to set out into the wild and wonderful world of investment, be it via stock market, property, or – wait for it – comic books.

Proper investing will take up a bit of money that you won't need for a while, but while it is not without risk, it needn't be too daunting. You just need to do some homework, and get your head around a few core concepts and terms. Once you've got the jargon down, you can confidently dive right in and start taking advantage of all the amazing opportunities out there.

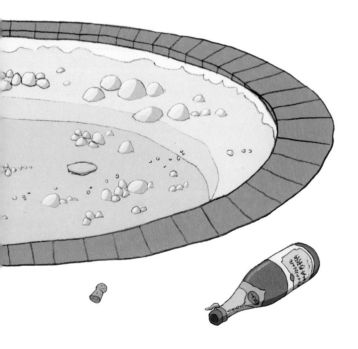

The Basics of Stock Market Investing

Investing is similar to saving, the difference is that there is a much higher risk element involved when you invest. If you are buying shares, for example, you are buying a fantastically small part of a company, and according to how this company performs, your original investment will rise or fall in value. This means you might not only make no profit, you could even lose your original investment.

If the public likes a company, and it is reaping profits as a result, then more people will want to buy shares in it, and the price of these shares will increase. It's the law of supply and demand.

In the UK, the behind-the-scenes work on share prices happens on the floor of the London Stock Exchange. Shares are bought by traders; they hold them and sell them off to investment companies at prices set by the market. The entire market system is really a sophisticated version of an auction.

Investments can be for medium or long term – from as little as five years to as long as you like, depending upon what you invest in. Investing in the stock market can be really thrilling, and you can get a proper kick out of watching your money grow. But before you start feverishly scanning the FTSE 100 every morning over your espresso, here are a couple of things to consider:

• There is no guarantee an investment will give a good return or even that you will get back the same amount you invested in the first place.

• Money that's invested needs to be left for at least a couple of years, so it shouldn't be money that might be needed suddenly or to pay off debts; it needs to be 'forgotten' for a while.

• Investing all your money in just one company because you love their products may seem like a good idea, but you might lose everything if their shares fall unexpectedly. Successful investors spread their financial eggs between several baskets to get a mix of different investment products.

Share ISAs

While cash ISAs (see the **Banking** chapter) are guaranteed tax-free savings, an ISA that invests in the stock market involves the risk of losing some (possibly all) of your money. However, it also offers much higher returns than with a cash ISA account. The annual limit on tax-free investment in a share ISA is £7,200. Investing into a share ISA is either by a lump sum up to the maximum, a lump sum with further investments up to the maximum, or in regular (such as monthly) installments. All sorts of investments can be wrapped in an ISA and any income or gains from them are completely tax-free. You can choose to buy a share ISA through a specialist adviser, a bank or a building society.

Types of Stock Market Investments

Investments in the stock market are generally known as investment funds and they come in a variety of shapes and colours. To give you an overview we've compiled a short list of the different investment types available. These explanations should give you a head start:

Unit trusts or Open-Ended Investment Companies (OEICs)

Unit trusts allow you to share in a pool of investments selected by a fund manager. Instead of buying shares, you buy units – the difference being that there are an unlimited or 'open-ended' number of units available, whereas in a company only a limited number of shares will ever be available.

The fund manager who runs the unit trust will buy shares in different companies; these are then pooled in a fund, and split into units. There are hundreds of unit trusts but each has a different investment strategy; some specialize in certain areas, such as science and technology or fashion.

Some unit trust funds allow you to begin with an investment of as little as £50. Investing a small amount of money on a regular basis, instead of a lump sum, spreads out the risk. Because the prices of units vary from month to month, some months you might feel like you've got a bargain, while at other times the units you've bought will fall in price.

You can buy Unit Trusts directly from the investment management company or through a financial adviser. Your money is looked after by an independent trustee who keeps a close eye on the company managing the fund.

→ **www.investmentuk.org** - The Investment Management Association explains all about OEICs and unit trusts.

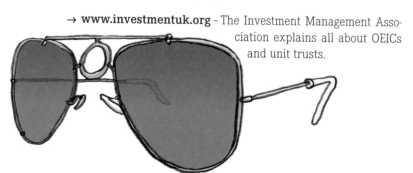

Index tracking

An index is a collection of shares designed to reflect the performance of a particular stock market, or part of it. The two main UK indexes are the FTSE 100 and the FTSE All Share.

The FTSE All Share tracks the share price of all the companies listed on stock market; the FTSE 100 tracks just the top 100 companies. There are other sub indexes including the FTSE 250 and the FTSE 350. For example, British Airways is listed on the FTSE 100 while a smaller company such as Burberry, the fashion label, would be included on the FTSE All Share. There are around 500 companies included on the FTSE All Share.

Index tracker funds follow a stock market index, automatically adjusting to take account of changes in that index. **Tracker funds are the UK's most popular collective stock market investment** and in the past 20 years they have done well.

→ **www.ftse.com** - Read more about the different indexes and the world's top companies.

→ **www.londonstockexchange.co.uk** - Find out more about shares and companies.

Bonds

Bonds are a relatively safe, stock-market-related investment. When a company issues a bond they are asking investors to help them pay back their debt, or to raise money for business plans, such as taking over another company. The company pays the investors interest, sometimes at a fixed rate. Some bonds also pay investors an income, either annually or monthly.

The only risk with a bond is if the company issuing it goes bust and can't pay back the money. The government also issues bonds – known as gilts – to raise money for public projects.

Investment trusts

Investment trusts buy shares in other companies; they tend to have a theme, such as technology or science. They are 'close-ended', which means there is only a limited number of shares, and they can be sold at a premium or a discount depending on how many are available. Investment trusts often have quite large charges. An investment trust will be listed on the stock market as a company – one whose sole business is buying shares, and whose value is based on the performance of other companies.

→ **www.theaic.co.uk** – The Association of Investment Companies sheds light on how investment trusts function.

Exchange Traded Funds (ETFs)

ETFs buy shares in companies and then list them on the stock market. They have very low charges, unlike unit trusts, and as an investor you don't pay stamp duty (tax on buying shares and property) on transactions. They track a particular index, for example the FTSE 100, and the fund gets bigger if more people invest and smaller if people withdraw their money.

Commodities

Not all pooled investment funds invest only in shares; some will also invest in commodities. A commodity is an everyday item – coffee, tea, corn, wheat, oil, gold –which is traded on all international stock markets at a price dependent on supply and demand. The price of commodities changes according to matters such as the weather and the environment – for example, the quest for alternative fuel is pushing up the price of corn and palm oil. When fund managers invest in commodities they are not actually buying the gold or oil directly; they are buying 'futures': agreements to buy a set amount of a particular commodity at a date in the future, but at a price set now.

Property funds

Property funds are for those who fancy dabbling in the property market, but don't necessarily have hundreds of thousands of pounds to spare. Options include:

• Unit trusts (or investment trusts) which invest in companies developing property. Most of these will be in companies developing new office space or building residential property to house workers or students. These are fairly risky so get specialist advice.

• Real Estate Investment Trusts (REITs) have only been around since 2006. They are a way to invest directly in actual property. Obviously investing in residential property can be tricky if there is a house-price crash, but REITs have a pool of different types of property that aren't usually as badly affected, such as student accommodation, nursing homes, car parks and shopping malls.

The money has to stay in the fund for at least three years, and you can invest as little as £5,000 (small beer where property is concerned). Like with other investments, you can wrap your REIT in an ISA or a Self-Invested Personal Pension (SIPP) and watch your money grow tax free.

→ **www.reita.org** - Information about property investment.

Capital Gains Tax

This is a tax everyone must pay if they make a capital gain – i.e. if you've made money on something like selling shares or property. There is a set amount of money you are allowed to make before paying tax on it; in 2007/2008 the CGT allowance was up to £9,200 per person. The allowance is reviewed annually in the Budget.

Ways to Invest Ethically

There's a common misconception that if you're eager to make your money work for you, ethics can't be a priority. But there is such a thing as ethical investment – and it's not all about tree-hugging, eating brown rice and wearing odd-shaped sandals. It's an astute financial policy.

There are several ways to invest with a good conscience. If you like a company, then you can support it by buying shares in it. If you like its policies and ethics, the chances are other people will too, which is all good news as you will make money if it does well. Another way of investing ethically is via something called 'Collective Investments'. This is putting money into specific funds which only invest in the shares of socially responsible companies.

The FTSE 4 Good

The FTSE 4 Good is similar to the regular FTSE (Financial Times Stock Exchange), but with an important difference: the FTSE 4 Good tracks the performance of companies adopting ethical practices worldwide. It was launched in 2001 by FTSE.

Before being chosen for inclusion in the list, a company has to have shown they are either in the process of working towards or have achieved all of the following five things:

• environmental sustainability
• positive relationships with stakeholders
• support for universal human rights
• good supply-chain labour standards, i.e. no child labour and no bonded labour
• anti-bribery policies

To ensure that the FTSE 4 Good remains ethical and that companies stick to their good practices, the list is updated regularly. The FTSE 4 Good inclusion criteria are also reviewed regularly and may be changed as social conditions change.

Speculation

A wise soul once said you have to speculate to accumulate, and fortunately speculation no longer generally entails scrabbling around with a gold pan in an icy creek in the Klondike. One of the nicest things about modern-day speculation is that providing you're comfortable with the amounts you're investing and the time and effort it takes, **working your hobbies and interests into your moneymaking schemes can be a real pleasure**.

A speculator is of the same species as an investor, but with slightly different habits. Speculation is riskier than conservative investment, and for that reason speculators need to be strategic about where they put their money. It's a DIY version of investment, in which, as well as putting some of your money into a risk-free savings account, you might also choose to take a chance on a painting, a hotel, or a natural resource. Here we take you through some forms of speculation.

Risk

Becoming finance savvy means being aware of boundaries – and knowing what your attitude is towards risk. Most financial experts agree that what determines this attitude is not how much money you have but where you are in life, and how much you are prepared and able to lose. No matter how much money someone has – be it millions or even billions – ill-informed speculation could see them losing everything. The rich usually stay rich by knowing exactly how much they can afford to lose and when to stop speculating.

The key is to acknowledge the risk inherent in speculation and spread it over different markets. If you have a mortgage, you basically already invest in property. If you have other money you want to invest, then it's sensible to pursue speculation in markets such as commodities, tech shares, or contemporary art dealing. This way, you'll have other investments to fall back on if one of the markets breaks down.

Speculating on property

There are three types of property investment: stock-market-based investments, which we mentioned earlier, buy-to-let investments and investing in your own home.

The last one may sound surprising but believe it or not **paying off your mortgage is one of the best property investments you can make.** Not only can it save thousands of pounds in interest, but the money saved can be put towards a simple savings account like an ISA, thereby saving tax payments in the process. Most mortgage lenders have offers that allow a certain amount to be overpaid each year, putting customers closer to owning their own home, faster (see **Mortgage** chapter for more details).

Buy-to-let

It seems like a great idea: buy a home, rent it out and watch the money roll in. If you can find an area where property is cheap, and where you can charge a reasonable rent, buy-to-let can be a worthwhile investment. To make this really work, you will ideally need about 25 per cent of the proposed property's value as a deposit. Then you need to be able to charge a rent of around 120 per cent of your mortgage repayments. This allows for extras such as paying a letting agent to rent out and manage the property, repairs and the risk of tenants who forget to pay their rent on time. Profit on a buy-to-let property consists of the yield made on the rent and the capital made on the price of the property itself. If you have the energy for this type of real-estate investment, making money through rising house value and tenant income can be a very lucrative financial venture.

→ **www.cml.org.uk/cml/consumers/guides/buytolet** - The Council of Mortgage Lenders. Check out the useful factsheet.

→ **www.arla.co.uk** - The Association of Residential Letting Agents has good advice for potential landlords.

Specialist Investments

Wine

A sure sign of wealth is a well-stocked wine cellar – and it's also a fantastic investment opportunity: returns on some classic vintages can top 10 per cent a year. Before getting carried away during the weekly shop to Tesco, bear in mind that all good wines need to be stored properly. Even the best wine can become worthless if left in a kitchen wine rack.

Like any investment, wine requires spreading your risk, so it's best to start off with one crate at a time of different sorts of wine. Knowing wine takes years of research and knowledge, so it's well worth investing some more money in taking a few wine courses, visiting a few vineyards (all in the cause of research of course) and really getting to know about your subject.

→ **www.decanter.com** - Find out more about collecting wine.

Furniture, limited editions and art and antiques

Classic cars, rare antiques and art, stamps, rare albums and first editions all count as investments – so long as someone is prepared to pay more than you spent on them. Not that you should wait for the *Antiques Roadshow* team to come to you: do your research, start collecting, hold onto those valuable collectibles and let them appreciate over time. For instance:

→ **www.ukphilately.org.uk** – Discover the world of stamp collecting here. It's big business.

For furniture, limited editions and art and antiques, get information on how to sell and what to look for at reputable auction sites:

→ **www.sothebys.com**
→ **www.christies.com**
→ **www.bonhams.co.uk**

The Secrets of Collecting

Quality Anything from furniture to toys should be in the best condition possible. In the case of artwork, you may have to budget enough money to cover restoration, maintenance and insurance costs. If you are collecting toys and computer games remember to keep the packaging – preferably leave them unopened: serious investors will pay good money for this alone.

Research There's no substitute for knowing exactly what you are buying. It's very easy to end up with a fake if you don't know your stuff, and no seller worth their salt will enlighten you if they know they're going to make good money out of your ignorance. There's no point becoming a collector unless you have a working knowledge of the subject or can afford a very good adviser. Use your own assets – you might fancy yourself as a collector of rare first editions, but if you don't know the first thing about original dust jackets, and can spot a 1973 Action Man at twenty paces, then you should be thinking about toy collecting instead.

Pleasure People will pay a lot of money for some very recent fads such as Beanie Babies, those Nat West piggy banks from the 1980s, original iMacs and even complete sets of Lego. It may be worth holding on to your PlayStation, Game Cube, BMX bikes, original Cluedo, classic edition DVDs and first print run CDs. After all, in a few years' time, when today's primary school children are running the major companies, they might just pay out top price in a bout of nostalgia.

One-offs Limited editions of almost everything collectable will increase an object's value, be it a specially labelled jar of Millennium Year Mustard or the first printing of *War and Peace*.

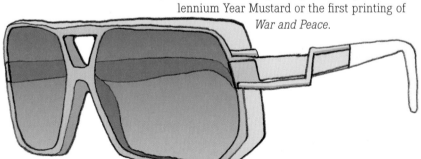

Invest in Yourself

Once your financial security is taken care of, the latent panic you've always felt about your future will give way to a warm self-confidence. In your daily life, you will notice that often your ability to afford an object of desire is already so satisfying that you don't actually need to buy it. Take pleasure in being able to say 'I can afford a Ferrari' rather than bragging about having just bought one.

Now you have the luxury of choice what to spend your extra money on (or not), be it the latest Nintendo gadget, a designer dog or a private jet. You can also decide to use your money for the good of others, paying for your sister's wedding, supporting the local animal shelter or funding research on alternative fuel products. Every choice you make is an investment in who you are. It's up to you.

Glossary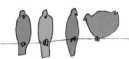

AER (Annual Equivalent Rate) The amount of interest you are paid on savings.

APR (Annual Percentage Rate) The amount of interest you will pay on a loan per year; it can be used to work out the total cost of taking out a loan, including administrative costs and other hidden extras.

BACS payments Bankers Automated Clearing Services. A way of moving money electronically from one account to another, and the method by which most employers pay their staff.

Base rate The interest rate set by the Bank of England once a month to maintain a stable financial system in the UK. Banks and building societies use it as a guide for the amount of interest they will pay or charge their customers.

Bond A high-interest account that locks your money away for a while. It is worth considering if you have any spare cash you're fairly certain you won't need for a while. Best not confused with ...

Balance The amount of money in an account. This can be either a positive balance, if you have money in the account, or a negative balance, if you owe money (i.e. an overdraft).

Balance transfer The act of moving a balance, either positive or negative, between accounts, such as when you take out a new credit card and move your debt from the old card to the new one.

Bond, James A secret agent with a taste for strong martinis, beautiful women and Swiss banks (also known as 007).

Budgeting Making sure that your monthly income and outgoings balance out.

Building societies Similar to banks but they are mutual companies, which means they are basically owned by their customers.

Buy-to-let A form of property investment in which a property is bought for the direct purpose of being let out to others.

Capital gains tax Tax paid on profit you make when you sell an investment such as shares or property.

Capped interest An interest rate that is fixed so it can't rise above a specified amount.

Child trust funds A lovely government savings and investment account that allows under 18 year olds to save tax-free.

Compound interest The interest that your interest earns if you leave your money in a savings account long enough.

Credit card A plastic card that allows you to spend money you don't yet have by borrowing it from a company and repaying it through monthly bills – with very high interest rates. Otherwise known as one of the most effective methods of getting into debt frighteningly fast.

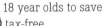

Collective investments (aka pooled investments) An investment where many people put different amounts of money into a fund. A fund manager, hopefully with a lucky hand, then invests this in one or more asset classes.

Commodities Basic resources and agricultural products such as sugar, soybeans, rice, wheat, gold and silver. Commodities are not only being traded in the supermarket around your corner but also in larger quantities on the world stock market.

Credit rating A measure of how much credit a lender will give you. It's based on a number of criteria, for example, your presence on the electoral roll and how reliable you have proven yourself at repaying your debts. Your credit rating can also affect the interest rate you are charged on a loan.

Credit unions Locally based lending and saving clubs that are run by members for members.

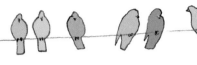

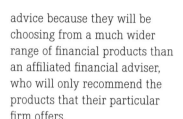

Debit card A piece of plastic that allows you to spend and withdraw money from your account (including any available overdraft).

Ethical banking Investing your money in an ethical manner. This could be through getting a credit card that donates a percentage of the interest to charity, investing in funds that are not tied to shady industries, or simply popping your wages in an account with an ethical bank.

Fixed-rate interest When the amount of interest you pay or are paid is set over a period of time.

FSA The Financial Services Authority, which regulates all businesses selling financial products.

advice because they will be choosing from a much wider range of financial products than an affiliated financial adviser, who will only recommend the products that their particular firm offers.

IHT (Inheritance Tax) A tax paid on any wealth that is left after someone dies, provided it exceeds the IHT threshold.

Index A collection of shares designed to reflect the performance of some part of, or even all of a particular stock market. The two main UK indexes are the FTSE 100 and the FTSE All Share.

Inflation The changing value of currency, or 'why everything is more expensive than it used to be'.

FTSE 4 Good An index that tracks the performance of companies adopting ethical practices.

IFAs (Independent Financial Advisers) Financial advisers who are not affiliated to a company. This means they will generally give you more impartial

Insurance Financial cover which pays out if the worst should happen.

Insurance excess In case of a claim, this is the nominal amount you will have to pay before you will receive money from the insurance company.

Insurance premium The fee for an insurance policy, which is usually paid annually or monthly.

Interest The money that lenders charge you for the privilege of borrowing from them.

Interest-free period A pleasing introductory offer where credit-card providers don't charge you interest for the first few months after taking out a card with them.

Interest-only mortgage A mortgage in which you only pay off the interest that is accruing on the loan, and the original amount borrowed remains untouched.

ISA (Individual Savings Account) An account that allows you to save a certain amount of money tax-free each year. There are cash ISAs and share ISAs.

Joint account A bank account that is used by several people.

Ken Young The chap who invented the sports sandal. It is unknown, however, whether or not Mr Young advocated wearing them with socks.

Mortgage An enormous loan that you take out in order to buy a property, and pay back over a long period of time.

National Savings & Investments (NS&I) The government-enacted savings bank. It provides savings accounts and runs premium bonds.

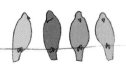

Interest rate The fee taken by a lender in exchange for giving you a loan. This is usually expressed as a percentage of the total amount that you have to pay back on top of what you originally borrowed.

Notice accounts Savings accounts that require you to give warning when you want to withdraw money.

Offshore banking Bank accounts in places where UK tax law doesn't apply, often in countries with excellent weather conditions. Normally used by non-UK taxpayers.

OFT (Office of Fair Trading)
Financial services are products, just like a Ferrari or a tin of beans. If you feel you have been misled or the product was substandard then you can complain to the Office of Fair Trading.

Overdraft The facility that allows you to spend more money than there is in your bank account.

Pension The money you save to keep you in your dotage, either through the state, your company, or a personal plan.

Private bank Normally used by high-income earners, provides convenient extras such as a stockbroker, financial advice and a posh-looking bankcard.

REIT (Real Estate Investment Trust) These invest in actual property instead of shares.

Repayment mortgage When you repay the entirety of the mortgage plus all the interest that it has accumulated, usually over a term of 25 years.

Retail Prices Index A domestic measure of inflation, or the decreasing value of money, which has been continuously available since June 1947. Many interest rates are linked to the RPI.

Savings account A bank account in which you earn more interest than with a current account for allowing your money to sit for a long period of time.

Shareholders People who own shares of a company.

Sharia banking Banking according to the five 'pillars' of an Islamic society: faith, life, wealth, intellect and posterity.

Standing Orders An arrangement by which money is debited automatically from your account on a regular basis.

Underwriter Not to be confused with undertaker, it is the financial institution guaranteeing the money the insurers will use to pay out a claim.

Unit trusts or Open-Ended Investment Companies (OEICs)
A form of collective investment: instead of buying shares, you buy units.

Valuation An inspection that a bank or building society will normally require is carried out on property before deciding whether to allow a mortgage for it. This is to make sure the property really is worth the bank's investment.

Variable-rate interest
Interest that fluctuates, normally according to the base-rate changes.

Acknowledgements

One name goes on the cover, but a book is always a team effort, this one as well. I am very grateful for the support that I have received from the lovely people around me. I owe special thanks to Caroline Blake and Matthias Megyeri, who both were absolutely indispensable in the development of the White Rabbit series. They generously helped from day one and have been patrons to the project ever since. I also want to thank Joly Braime, who helped to maintain the humorous tone that he instilled throughout the Debt title.

Furthermore, I want to thank the following people, who all contributed to the success of this publication: Claire Andrews, Philip Borel, Jane ní Dhulchaointigh, Suzanne Earl, Bryony Fox, Marion Gillet, Katalin Hausel, Henry Herkner, David Inman, Alex Marshall, Dr Andreas Otterbach, Barbara Otterbach, Carolin Otterbach, Christiane Otterbach, Ulrich Otterbach, Andrew Perkins, Liz Prescott, Henrietta Rose-Innes, Paula Saunders, Kelly Thompson, and Laura Williams.

When the White Rabbit series was still at idea stage, Otterbach & Partners was granted an award by the National Endowment for Science, Technology and the Arts (NESTA). Through NESTA's support, in particular Hugo Manassei, Siân Prime, Mark Fenwick and Mark Elliott, we were able to develop this new series.

The following experts kindly agreed to read through individual chapters of the book and check whether any factual mistakes had sneaked in: Colin Jackson and Michael Brill of Baronworth, Kevin Carr of Lifesearch, Margaret Robertson and Rachel Vahey.